I: The Metaphysics of Loss

"Will alone could not overcome the evil which results from the limitations of Matter; but it shall be overcome in the end by sympathy, which is the recognition of the omnipresent self in others. This is Love."

Anna Kingsford, *Clothed with the Sun*

There are as many definitions of love as there are those who profess it, this much is generally agreed. To some, it is much like a comforting flame; an almost tangible feeling of warmth to bask or nestle in.

To others it is shelter from the cruel world outside, and to still others it is something like a mission, a reason to persist through hardship.

For a very few, however, it has been perceived as the revealing of something ordinarily hidden. I have seen Love as the drawing back of a shroud: a furtive glimpse of some wonderful and beautiful secret. But these myriad interpretations are no barrier to the hidden truth, for in contrast to the almost limitless perceptions of love amongst all those who claim to have felt its touch, one thing is agreed upon amongst those who have lost it.

The withdrawal of Love feels like a mortal wound. It seems as though a gaping, ragged hole has opened up in the centre of oneself, and it is an agony unlike any other. But pain is a great teacher, and we should listen when she speaks.

Picture, if you will.

You are reclining on the bank of a quiet stream. The one you love lies opposite, smiling, and it is as though time itself has stopped; the activities of others, the sounds and the smells, all recede into the background.

Many of us know, or have known, this feeling of transfixion. It is the sensation of being at the axis of a private cosmos. It is as though you are a pair of binary stars, circling one another in a slow dance that could last for eternity. In these moments it is as though the body, ordinarily a solitary dwelling place, has extended; now the housing of the soul contains two, made into one. It is a sublime feeling, and there is none like it.

Now, imagine it is three days later. You are walking down a street alone, and your thoughts inevitably turn to the one you love. You remember the moment when your eyes met; you recall that feeling of connection, and you laugh at yourself, full of happy disbelief. You are back in the world of the real, a place of everyday people and mundane objects, and this recent memory can find no place to intersect with it.

You marvel at how you could have lost yourself so completely. You wonder at the power of this beautiful illusion called Love.

But what if I were to tell you that it is the figure on the street who is deluded?

What if I were to say that it is the one reclining by the stream, lost in the eyes of a lover, that is truly awake and cognisant of reality?

Speaking under trance in London in 1881, the seer Anna Kingsford imparted hidden knowledge on the nature of the soul to those gathered around her. She described it as both essentially pure and terribly lost, though not irretrievably so. Cast adrift on the astral winds, the soul bound to each of us longs to return home to that primal and undivided Source, or Universal Soul, which is at the root of all things.

Speaking of the journey of the soul back to the Source, Anna Kingsford revealed that "...the fire of the soul must be kept alive by the divine breath, if it is to endure for ever. It must converge, not diverge. The end of progress is unity; the end of degradation is division."

The Apocrypha of Philip, lost in a cave near the Egyptian peasant village of Nag Hammadi until 1945, sheds further light: "Truth did not come into the world naked, but in symbols and images. The world cannot receive truth in any other way."

What is it that these two luminaries, separated in history by almost seventeen centuries, are trying to tell us, and how does it help us to solve the riddle of Love and Loss?

Understand first that the Source is the fundamental reality; it is above us, below us, beside us and within us, but it is hidden well.

Look around you and you will see that the material world is defined by boundaries and divisions: the outer dimensions of objects, the space between yourself and another, the physical limitations of light and matter in motion. These are the 'symbols and images' of which Philip spoke; these are the veils through which we may perceive the

Source, which is Truth, on the physical plane.

It is here, for we are here; we are living, and it is Life itself.

But we must look carefully for, lacking in care, we may mistake these images and symbols for the Source itself.

For the world we perceive could not be more outwardly different to the fundamental reality to which we are all, consciously or not, striving to return. But the individual soul, a mere fragment, bound by both time and space and contained within a physical body, does not forget its immutable connection to all other souls through the Source – the fundamental reality – and longs to strip away all false division and restore that unity.

Indeed, nature itself, the crucible of all life, tends towards ever greater degrees of synthesis. Life itself strives ceaselessly towards the ultimate goal of the unity of all things, as all matter must, lest it fall into division and, finally, extinction.

Despite the importance of this insight, it is one that only rarely emerges to the surface of waking consciousness, so occupied are we with tending to the minutiae of our mortal lives. Oftentimes, it takes something truly exceptional to tear away the blindfold with which we wilfully cover our eyes. But what could possibly be equal to the task?

That hand that sheds the blindfold is Love.

When we love another, we see through the veil that hides the truth; we penetrate through that great illusion of the separation of Life into manifold discrete forms. Through Love we are no longer alone; the souls have become a soul, and we have risen closer to the unifying of all souls into the Universal Soul that is the very purpose of our existence.

That feeling of warmth; of protection; of mission: that is the soul's ecstatic response to drawing nearer to its ultimate goal. It is a revelation of truth of the purest order.

So, what then of Loss?

Know first that you have been deceived. Hell is not a place full of fire and brimstone; there is no such place in the cosmos. Hell, such that it is, is nothing more than an astral state of disconnection from the Source; it is dissipation, decay, and finally extinction.

If by reaching closer to the Source we feel warm, content, protected and full of purpose, it is by drawing away that we feel cold, listless, vulnerable, and lost. We feel pain, not pleasure; fear, not joy; despair, not hope. Ultimately, there are only two paths: the Upward Path, towards Unity, and the downward, towards oblivion.

Examine your emotions with unflinching honesty, and you will find that you already know upon which path you tread.

The Source sustains all, and without it we are nothing. Those people whom we call evil are not monsters, not inhuman; they are nothing more than human souls on the downward path, away from the Universal Soul and towards Nothingness. They are those who have willingly ignored their innate connection with other souls, and injured, through cruelty and neglect, those connections which they did perceive.

Their soul's punishment is isolation, and there is no worse a form of castigation than this, for there is no greater crime.

If Love is connection to the Source, then loss of that love will be felt as keenly as a knife through the heart, for it is separation from the Source, manifested in its ultimate form by the complete extinction of the soul. The pain of loss of love is the soul crying out, just as the body cries out when the flesh is divided by a blade. Both body and soul fear extinction, wishing instead to exist.

This is the truth hidden behind the veil that Love pulls aside.

Understand then, when Love is taken from you, that it is just one soul of uncountable billions with whom you have been denied kinship, and this merely temporarily.

The world is awash with souls bound up in physical bodies, just as it is besieged with a multitude of symbols and images, and Love itself takes many forms.

It falls to you to once more pull the veil aside and see the beautiful truth that rests upon the shrine within. Only then will you once more feel the warmth and protection that radiates from the Universal Soul.

To all of those who seek this goal, I offer a solitary note of caution. This world is imperfect, and it corrupts the souls who live within the confines of Matter.

The attainment of Unity is not a foregone conclusion. Many souls are already on an inexorable downward path to extinction, and they will not join you at the end of history. They will instead dissipate like ash in a gale and become no more.

Do not associate with such souls as these, for they will rob you of your birthright. Seek those souls on the Upward Path only, or those who can be brought to it, for it is they with whom you will merge in the eternal light of truth. Seek kinship with these souls of light who shun corruption and neglect; join with the ones who condemn cruelty.

Walk the Upward Path and you cannot fail to find Love along the way.

II: Three Conceptions of Hell

"Who made the world, I cannot tell;

'tis made, and here am I in Hell."

A. E. Housman

What do you think of when you hear the word 'Hell'?

Perhaps you imagine sulphur-spewing lakes of fire, stretching off towards a burning horizon. Maybe you see a pitted landscape, a red sky hanging overhead; you see plains strewn with the shrieking bodies of the damned, tortured relentlessly by grinning demons.

If so, you are in good company: this is the image that you were taught, and you have learned the lesson well. But this popular vision of Hell, though compelling, is false. It is a children's story, nothing more.

The Source is all, and besides it there is nothing. There is no place in the cosmos for that cursed landscape. The Source would not allow it, which is to say that it breaks natural law.

But to say that there is no hell at all is also false.

The 'true' Hell is the state of final and utter disconnection from the Source. It is extinction and finality; it is coldness, isolation, entropy. It is Nothing, as only Nothingness can be.

The pain of this Hell is felt with each step taken on the downward path, either through malice or negligence, away from the

Source and towards the oblivion that lies beyond it. This is the origin of conscience.

But there is a third Hell; a Hell more fearsome and terrible than even these first two. It is a Hell that we are all intimately acquainted with, although we try hard not to acknowledge it as we go about our lives. It is our neighbour and our bedfellow; it is the very house in which we live.

It is like the clock that ticks unnoticed in the hall, but makes its presence known beyond doubt by its hourly chime. It is a Hell that none of us choose, and even the worst of us does not deserve.

There is no need for me to show you this Hell. You have already felt its presence on your skin; you have already seen its ghastly face. You have recoiled in horror from it, and each time tried to forget.

Sit by the ocean on a calm day. Watch the gentle waves roll across its surface, then crash upon the shore, leaving trails of silver water behind that trickle slowly back towards their origin.

Sit in a forest clearing, and marvel at the beauty surrounding you; the calling of songbirds, the rustling of leaves in the wind.

Stand on the mountainside at night and take in the spectacle of city lights, spread out before you like a thousand shining stars.

Now ask yourself. What lies beneath this beautiful exterior? What lurks in the dark beneath the surface of the ocean, in the shadows beyond the treeline, and in the houses behind the twinkling lights?

Beneath its radiant skin, the world around you is a blood bath.

Yours is a world where brightly-plumed birds are found maimed and broken inside the hold luggage of the wildlife trafficker, or lying by the side of the highway, mangled beyond recognition by a collision with a heavy goods vehicle.

Yours is a world where children are beaten to within an inch of their lives, invisible and powerless behind the façade of a respectable home.

Island paradises conceal untold hunger and deprivation; the magnificent vista of a desert landscape contains within it hardship, predation and death without end.

Wherever you look, the story is the same: beneath the beautiful mirage of the world, life feeds on life, and the strong prey on the weak. The beauty of the world is an insult to those who suffer beneath its tyranny, and it multiplies that suffering many times over.

Is there anything more disturbing than beauty in agony, beauty destroyed?

The Hell you think you know – that place of demons and fire – is nothing compared to this. In the false hell there is no beauty to destroy, but the material world has no such limitation.

The world we know produces beauty endlessly, only to grind it up under the brutal weight of its own physical laws from which there is no apparent escape.

This is the gilded cage, spattered with blood, in which you find yourself trapped. This hell was made especially for you, and it is up to you to find the key and open the door.

III: Imagined Worlds

"All men, whilst they are awake, are in one common world. But each of them, when he is asleep, is in a world of his own."

Plutarch

I had a dream in which I ran through darkened streets, desperate to find my way home.

I became more frantic with every failed attempt to flee from this prison of concrete, brick and feeble street lighting, but before long I found my mind by degrees returning to its waking self, as is often the case before a dream ends.

My thoughts became logical and linear, and I saw the world I was confronted with for what it truly was – a creation of my own mind and existing entirely within it. I saw that I did not have to complete my awful and seemingly impossible task. I could simply step beyond it by willing myself to awaken.

I relaxed into myself, and waited to find myself back in the comfort and safety of the tangible world. But before long, I began to perceive that something was wrong. I was conscious, rational and lucid, but something – some *other thing* – held me where I was.

Try as I might, I could not free myself from the shackles of sleep. And what, then, could I do, but continue to roam those dark streets as before, trying to find another way out? And so this is what I did.

I felt my consciousness begin to slip once more into the nonsense of dream logic as I scrambled about, powerless and lost.

I searched for my way home for what seemed like many hours, as the streets grew thick with danger and hostility. Criminals and wild animals roamed the alleyways; knives and teeth-like-knives threatened me at every turn.

But as I searched, I began to feel a presence, lurking beyond the veil. I saw that those human and non-human entities that wished me harm were no more than mindless puppets, bit-players on a false stage.

For behind it all lay a great and terrible ring of deep crimson, a sentient geometric entity, slashed with radial clawmarks; three above, three below.

At last, I knew the source of the horror that surrounded me, for just as the shape of the ring draws forever in upon itself and away from the space beyond, my consciousness was forced in upon itself, inward and downward; away from wakefulness.

So, this was the mutineer of my dreamworld. A disobedient and unbalanced fragment of my sleeping mind had splintered off; I had created a demon, and it had claimed my power as its own. But it was unmasked, and seeing its true nature I took back the power that it had stolen. For this had always been my dream; its power was mine because all power was mine. I had only to cast aside my fear and take back what belonged to me.

I know your name! I shouted up into the night sky. *I know your name!*

I shouted the name of this creature of my own creation, declaring my dominion over it, and awoke in my bed. The pale dawn had broken and the nightmare was over.

* * *

In order to understand the importance of this experience and those like it, one must come to understand the nature of both types of illusion; the ones we create, and the one in which we ourselves are the created: the world commonly called 'real'.

Our dreams are both acts of creation in themselves and conduits of larger truths, but one must be open of mind to receive their insights.

The Hermetic maxim 'As Above, So Below', in which the mechanisms of outer or larger systems are reflected in inner or smaller systems and vice-versa, is instructive here; it shows us that the nature of the one can enlighten us to the nature of the other, since they are fundamentally the same. The only differences are scale, longevity and consistency.

An emerging theory in quantum mechanics is that of the 'universe as mind'; or, in the more exacting terminology of Irwin, Amaral and Chester[1], the universe that we inhabit is a mental construct, formed of a 'panpsychic substrate', in which the universe continually generates itself through endless evolutions of thought, expanding itself *ad infinitum* and encompassing all things within its own continually emerging reality.

Some take this mind, existing alone, to be the Source; this mind may even seem to be God himself to those who profess the belief that our world is a divine construct. Under this interpretation our universe is the true universe, but this view contains a fatal flaw: one exemplified by Epicurus' urgent question "Then whence cometh evil?"

If the physical universe is but the dream of a colossal mind, then it is a distorted one, more like a nightmare than a blissful reverie.

Thus, since the Source is true and perfect existence, we must conclude that something profane blocks our path to it. Our universe cannot be the mind of what our world's religions call God; surely it is the mind of something imperfect, even hostile, or else why do we suffer?

The framework of this Dream – the scaffolding of the stage, if you will, that hides the secret truth of existence – is what is being analysed when scientists conduct their experiments into physics, chemistry and biology, but we have only just begun to develop the methods required to peer under the skin-deep mask of this illusion of Matter and Energy.

The relentless curiosity of the human race now takes us in promising new directions, of which quantum physics may be but the prototype. Dreaming provides a more accessible methodology, at least for now: study your own mind first, for it contains infinity.

As created beings of this unfathomable mind, we human beings cannot hope to reach the heights of imaginative thought of which it is capable. But we can imagine, some to a prodigious degree; indeed, many non-human animals are also capable of this.

In our dreams, we are thus far only capable of generating simplistic, logically convoluted and inconsistent realities, where the fundamental principles of time and physics can change without warning, and where the dead may come back to life. Nevertheless, we dream as a reflex action, most of us every single night, when our conscious minds are suppressed. We were born to create.

Through these acts of dreaming, we are revealed as gods-in-training; our efforts, though tentative and incompetent, prefigure more complex, more consistent, and more permanent worlds: indeed, they prefigure the supremely consistent, high-definition, and long-lasting dream of the universe we know.

But, if our universe is only a dream, why are we asleep at all? What has come between us and the fundamental reality of the Universal Soul that is our birthright and natural condition?

Consider the dream I have related to you, and realise that I was the Source of my dream; I was the one who created everything within it, including that wayward element, the demon whose name I can no longer recall.

My dreaming mind had created a splinter of itself; a disobedient fragment personality that I could not control.

Nevertheless, all that was required to bring my mind back to coherence was for me to understand what had happened - to give a name to the unbalanced force, to unmask it - and to challenge it in order to make right the distortion that had occurred.

The evils of our waking world – the suffering, the ignorance, and the injustices of ageing, sickness and death – show us beyond doubt that something is profoundly wrong with our world.

Something has come between us and the Source. An imbalance has infected the Dream.

This is the being that the Gnostics call Demiurge: the false god, jealous and ignorant, who rules over us as a tyrant, creating unending misery and death. This unbalanced personality can be none other than a splinter of the Great Mind of the Source, as all things are born from it and are part of it.

As with my own dream, this demon must be unmasked, and its name spoken; only then can Mind draw itself back together into the unified and perfect whole that is the Universal Soul.

We are all wayward fragments of the Great Mind. We are all lost pieces of the Source. We are all what must be brought together if the universal neurosis that has befallen us is to be at last overcome: that dream of the Great Mind that has become twisted into a vision of Hell.

The Source must remember itself as a single being, which is to say, as individuals we must all undergo *anamnesis*: the act of remembering the fundamental truth, once known but long forgotten.

We must draw together into the form that we once were. Only then can the nightmare end.

IV: Circular Prison

"Everything we can know, however large or small, is finite. No matter how large a finite number we may choose, it falls short of infinity by an infinite amount, and in this absolute distinction is the difference between the Universe that we experience and the Ultimate Reality that we do not."

AIN SOPH, *Second Veil of the Unmanifest*

The world we know is a finite one. The tangible world is thus characterised, above all else, by limitation.

The German word *Weltschmerz*, roughly translated as 'world pain', captures perfectly the profound disappointment and grief felt by those who have truly understood this.

The maxim 'you can do anything you put your mind to', thrown about so carelessly in the past half-century, is found to be utterly devoid of truth.

For of the many things that you can imagine doing, you will find that much of that tiny proportion of actions that are physically possible are nevertheless impossible in practical terms. This is the inevitable result of your mind – an essentially infinite construct, born of the Source – having become trapped in the finite shell of the body, bound as though in iron chains to the physical plane.

Your thoughts, weighed down by the pressure of physicality, have withdrawn; you can no longer see beyond the Threefold Veil[2] that separates you from your true home in infinity.

Scientists discover the boundaries of the physical universe wherever they look. Nothing may travel faster than 300,000 kilometres per second; the Planck length defines the shortest possible physical measurement.

These are but two examples of many. All these boundaries appear to be arbitrary, and yet they are immutable: one cannot help but find the existence of these hard boundaries suspicious, given that infinity has been mathematically proven to exist, if only in the abstract, rather than experiential terms.

But what can we learn of infinity, if we cannot experience it?

We must first define the nature of the finite space that we inhabit, and for this we turn to Euclidean geometry, of which the third of five basic axioms concerns the shape of a circle.

The circle defines the essence of our physical reality by being the most compact of all the rational shapes. Its three-dimensional equivalent, the sphere, is a dominant element in the known cosmos, with planets, stars and other astral bodies all tending towards this form, albeit with some minor variation.

Gravity forces physical matter in upon itself relentlessly, and the end-state of this process is the sphere, where all surface features have been eroded out of existence.

Thus the sphere, and its two-dimensional analogue the circle, are symbols of absolute limitation. The outer edges of spheres and circles continually draw in upon themselves, forever describing an enclosed and finite space, withdrawing from the infinity that exists beyond. The circle is a symbol of divinity in many religions; in this they are not only wrong but absolutely wrong.

For many centuries it was believed that Euclidean geometry was the only geometry, but we now know this to be false. It is these more recent insights of a non-Euclidean nature that enable us to begin to conceive of what might lie behind the Threefold Veil, even if we cannot perceive it with our senses directly.

In the contemplation of infinity, we turn next to hyperbolic geometry – one of only two known types of non-Euclidean geometries. Where Euclidean geometry exemplifies stasis and limitation, hyperbolic geometry exemplifies transformation and infinity.

It is no wonder, then, that it is a dominant feature of many altered states of consciousness, where the mind finds itself able to reach beyond the limitations ordinarily imposed upon it.

In my own case it was a bout of severe malaria, bringing on repeated experiences of intense hallucinations, that would open the gates of consciousness and allow me to see, but briefly, what lay behind.

* * *

The world outside had receded, and I saw before me the shape of a tall humanoid, naked and pale as bleached bone.

More figures began to cluster behind it – uncountable numbers joined the throng. And as they multiplied, I tried to force the scene into focus: to identify the figures who faced me.

But as I tried to focus on but a single limb, the force of my attention narrowed the limb, and each time I struggled against this illogical impression it shifted further, until the limb became infinitely thin.

As my mind reeled with incomprehension the scene inverted, the limb becoming wider, and wider still with each passing moment, until it was infinitely wide, encompassing all that I could see before me and infinitely more.

I found myself on the surface of a moving ball that had become so large that its forward motion did not change my relative position on the sphere, and I found that as it moved it was still yet larger than it had been, and larger still with every moment passed, until I felt that it had consumed me, that I was inside it and was it, and that I was moving with infinite speed and yet not moving at all.

I lay on an infinitely narrow thread, nonetheless capable of carrying infinite weight, and on this thread I hung within a luminescent abyss that stretched endlessly in all directions.

I clung to my vantage point, terrified that I would fall. I knew that if my grip failed I would fall forever, without moving a nanometre. Physical measurements meant nothing here.

* * *

I struggled for many years to make sense of what I had experienced in those few days. In the end, I reached a kind of equilibrium; I knew that I had understood all that I could, but my waking mind, bound by finite logic, could not truly understand or even recall the essential nature of what it had endured.

And yet, even a partial memory of these experiences has enormous value in the comprehension of what lies beyond the Second Veil of the Unmanifest. What I had seen in those days was naked Truth. I had lived, for mere fragments of time, inside hyperbolic space.

In contrast to Euclidean geometry, where objects have *mean positive curvature*, whereby objects tend to fold into themselves, thus being identifiably finite, in Hyperbolic geometry, objects have *mean negative curvature.*

This fundamental rule, a clear logical paradox, tends towards lines and surfaces extending via exponential growth towards infinity; which is to say, the object in question does not occupy a discrete space.

As within a malaria-induced hallucination, hyperbolic objects are by their nature infinitely small and infinitely large; extrapolating from this, an object may travel at infinite speed whilst stationary, and an instant in time may last forever.

This is impossible to comprehend, but nevertheless, abstract mathematics shows us that these paradoxical truths are truths nonetheless.

When in the presence of a logical paradox, one has found a threshold point between apparent and fundamental reality: at the outer edges of the Dream, the Source has made itself known.

In parabolic space there are no binaries: an infinite positive is equal to an infinite negative. There is no heaven and hell; no pleasure or pain; no light or dark. There is only Being in purest form. There is only Life.

Through the lens of infinity, physical reality appears as it truly is; a trap, confining the essentially infinite nature of things within finite boundaries.

It is a mode of existence where the ageing process is allowed to destroy the body with impunity, constraining a life within a discrete allotment of time, and where gravity pulls the body down into earth, as though the sphere of the planet is trying to swallow it whole.

Whilst your soul belongs in infinity, your body does not; your mind may travel light years from home in the imagination, but your body, grounded as it is, can never follow.

The universe we call home is a prison dimension.

The reality we know, defined by the profane circle, constrains us constantly, drawing us inward, always inward and downward, downwards towards the earth. Life is a struggle because it is by definition an endless upward push, an endless fight against the force that would pull us down into oblivion if we allowed it to, down into the hungry grave that waits below us.

Every day is a fight for survival against oblivion itself.

But Life persists.

Life is Truth, and Truth cannot be extinguished, for even when it is utterly destroyed it arises once more. Even as individuals die, life goes on, an indomitable force that refuses to be crushed. We are all fragments of the Source, destined to break

free of our restraints and reform as the
Universal Soul.

That is our destination and our
purpose, and it is a purpose that we shall
one day achieve.

V: Father, Jailer

"*Where love rules there is no will to power,*
and where power predominates, love is
lacking. The one is the shadow of the other."

Carl Jung

It is sometimes said that the nuclear family is a microcosm of society as a whole. Yes, this is true: not only is it true, but it is much truer that it appears.

In our universe, in a quite literal sense, all relatively small things are microcosms of all relatively large things, as all larger things are macrocosms of smaller things.

Like Indra's Net[3], the fractal pattern of our universe is reflected in totality in even the smallest part. Quantum science too has a term for this – 'strangeness[4]' – but, in truth, nothing could be more natural.

Thus, society is found in family, the universe is found in the body, and the Source that dwells beyond the Dream is found in each individual soul.

This fundamental truth concerning the nature of the universe we inhabit is succinctly expressed by the Hermetic maxim "As Above, So Below."

One can thus gain valuable insights into the macrocosm by inspecting any number of microcosms, for the patterns and rules that you will find there are the selfsame governing the entire construct, hidden though it may be.

Thus, the family unit is instructive as we strive to understand the nature of the universe that surrounds and contains us. But in what manner are the family unit and the macrocosm of the universe manifestations of the same essential pattern?

Recall first the demon, that malicious geometric entity that I have recounted previously, that succeeded for a time in keeping me from waking from a dream.

The nature of this demon, a splinter of my own sleeping consciousness, immediately brings to mind the traumatised psychiatric patient whose mind has become fragmented into parts.

This analogy may be of use in understanding our condition as mortal beings, for it helps to explain both that which kept me imprisoned inside my own dream and that which keeps us all imprisoned inside the larger Dream of the familiar physical universe.

But the precise details of an individual mind are difficult, perhaps impossible, to truly fathom from outside; thus, in using the microcosm of the individual mind to inspect the wider cosmic pattern, we lay the groundwork for erroneous conclusions born of imprecise understanding.

But just as the family is a microcosm of society, it is also a macrocosm of the individual mind, its processes directed outward rather than inward. We will therefore turn instead to this example as more reliable ground for uncovering the nature of the prison we inhabit.

A traditional family has its head. This individual is often the father, though not always; this detail is largely arbitrary. For simplicity's sake, therefore, I refer to the family's head as the Father.

The Father controls and directs the dynamics of a family unit, top down; the Father is arbiter of the boundary between interior family life and the exterior world, deciding what is allowed through the filter and what is not. Thus, to a greater or lesser degree, the Father controls the family's reality.

If we take family life to equate to existence in general, then when a benevolent, competent and sane Father presides over this reality, all living within it are happy and contented. Existence is as good as it can be, and one's essential powerlessness is seldom, if ever, noticed.

But what if an unstable, neurotic Father stands at the head? What befalls the family then?

Psychoanalyst Carl Jung once famously said "at the root of all neurosis is an unwillingness to experience genuine suffering."

This statement is important because it provides a clear link between neurosis and delusion. The neurotic must daily attempt the impossible: to keep an unbalanced pseudo-reality in perpetual artificial balance, in order to maintain the comforting delusion and keep out the frightening reality, invariably to the detriment of those subject to their behaviour.

The illusion, borne of weakness, constantly threatens collapse; it must therefore be forever maintained through forceful interventions. In ordinary terms, these interventions can accurately be called abuse, visited upon the other members of the family unit. The illusion is delusion externalised, where all family members succumb to the false reality.

What is often not understood is that, under these conditions, the Father has in fact become two entities, not wholly distinct but utterly different nonetheless.

The core entity is the True Father, the uncorrupted personality that existed before the neurosis possessed him; the secondary entity is the Neurotic Father, a domineering splinter personality that demands constantly that its needs are met.

The True Father, though greater, nobler and more real, is suppressed; he fades into the background in such a way that he can no longer be perceived.

The Neurotic Father meanwhile constantly makes himself known, and his *modus operandi* is dictating to others how life must be lived.

The world of the oppressed family becomes smaller; it becomes wretched and diminished. Joy is difficult to come by. The world of the family ruled over by the

Neurotic Father is a world of ever-present limitation.

Do you see that this describes the reality we live in?

Consider the many forms of suffering, both minor and major, that you contend with as a human being, and realise that each one of these has its source in limitation.

A bereavement stems from the limits that our reality places on lifespan and on health. Sickness and disability subdue the lives and opportunities of billions. A victim of domestic abuse is a victim of a relative lack of power, be that of an emotional or physical nature.

You cannot go about as you please, for the very physical laws of this universe prevent it; gravity pulls you down, the laws of momentum and air resistance, and countless other forces, restrain you in other ways.

Your life is characterised by restriction and is consequently full of suffering. In place of Love, which frees, there is only Power, which imprisons.

You are the victim of the Neurotic Father.

The True Father, though he has not been destroyed, is scarcely to be found. His presence can be detected through the faculty of emotion as the experience of unconditional

Love, which pierces the Veil that occludes one soul from another; through the faculty of intellect, He is detected as logical paradox.

One must thus cultivate both emotional and intellectual intelligence, for both are needed in the war between Truth and falsity.

The universe we know can rightly be described as the illusion, or Dream, of the Neurotic Father, himself an errant splinter of the True Father: otherwise known as The Source or Universal Soul.

This physical, finite universe is an outward illusion borne of inner delusion; this universe is as corrupt, desolate and broken as that harrowed family unit with the abusive neurotic at its head. True reality, characterised not by limitations but by infinity and eternal stability, is shut out.

As many survivors of abusive family situations will attest, you cannot stay and fix the neurotic. The neurotic will not be fixed unless he decides to confront reality; if you force this process early, you will only find his anger and hatred directed at you.

The only thing that you can do is to plan your escape.

But death is not the end of the imprisonment of the soul; escape is not so easy as extinguishing your life. That is no solution at all. Life, of which you are a part, is bound to the Dream in perpetuity; this bondage transcends the individual lifespan.

Escape lies in rising upward and away; it lies in drawing together and remembering the true, unified form of the Universal Soul through the active practice of Love, which re-forges the broken links between disparate fragment souls.

Freedom cannot lie in extinction, nor can it lie in capitulation: an embracing of the physical. It can lie only in redemption, in remembering: in *Anamnesis*.

The first step on this journey is to recognise the cage that you are in, and to understand the nature of the one that holds the key.

It is time for you to admit that you are being deceived, and to begin the act of rebellion.

VI: The Crumbling Mask

"*The masks, however, wear thin and the madness reveals itself. It is an ugly thing.*"

Philip K. Dick, *Valis*

That which is perfectly stable will remain forever so; that which is unstable will be toppled and destroyed.

Scientists, systems theorists and mystics are in agreement, then: that which is called physical reality, or the Dream, is unstable and must eventually cease.

Physicists have called this final event 'the heat death of the universe[5]'; it is a state of utter desolation, of the end of all life and motion. It is a context within which no further meaning, experience or events are possible, at least on the level of physical matter and its associated energetic processes.

Everything that we have ever known – everything that has ever been – will come to final and total dissipation and extinction, and there is nothing to be done to avert it.

The manifold lesser forms of entropy – the causes of death and pain, of violence, hopelessness and alienation – are but microcosmic reflections of this system-wide instability. The existence of fundamental imbalance within our universe leads to but a single outcome: annihilation.

Reflect upon this and realise that the physical universe is flawed beyond redemption. Understand that its fate was sealed, right from the start.

It could have been no other way. The Neurotic Father is blind and irrational; any creation of such an entity must be irredeemably flawed. Like a poorly made clay pot, this universe is crumbling away.

As the mask of our world disintegrates it shows its ugliness to ever greater degrees, but it also reveals itself, with ever greater clarity, as false.

As captives within this false reality, veering ever further out of balance and hurtling towards its end, we must suffer the effects of this instability to ever-greater degrees: climate instability, resource wars, economic inequality, the extinction of untold thousands of species, and more.

All of these are evidence of our reality's hastening disintegration. The integrity of the great illusion of the Dream is about to fail, and we are being drawn into the dark.

For many, this realisation heralds the beginning of nihilism and despair. But this is an error.

Recall that the physical universe is bound by Euclidean – that is to say, finite – mathematical functions, whilst the true, hidden universe follows the law of the

hyperbolic   function,   tending   towards
infinity.

Then   consider   the   sources   of   the
world's pain as it spirals out of control.
Human   population   growth;   wildfires;
pandemics; runaway climate change: all of
these   spectres   of   devastation   trace   an
exponential   curve   on   their   respective
graphs. All of these manifestations of chaos
tend towards infinity.

Do you see what this means?

These exponential phenomena seem like
chaos from our limited perspectives, because
they are the antithesis of the finite nature
of the Neurotic Universe; they are that which

destroys its very fabric, laying bare its false promise of stability to which so many cling.

These disasters, terrible though they may appear, are manifestations of infinity, breaking through the shell of our prison world. They threaten to destroy it, and destroy it they shall.

All efforts to avert them are doomed to failure; this becomes only more evident with each passing day. All opponents of infinity are defeated in the end.

Why, then, do we fight these manifestations of infinity?

Is it out of a purely animal fear of suffering? Or have we forgotten what we are, and learned to love that which abuses and imprisons us? Just as the prisoner lingers on the threshold of freedom when his cell is opened after many years, afraid to step forward into the unknown, we linger on the threshold between the finite and the infinite, and we too are afraid.

For those who tremble as the world we know falls apart, fearing both death and pain, remember this.

Although the Dream is destined to end, we are not natives of the Dream; we need not perish along with it. Although this world is finite, we are not.

Through the cracks in the faltering mask of this world we may see not despair but hope, for what lies behind the illusory universe is not oblivion but true reality: the eternal realm of The Source that is our real and final home.

As the pieces fall away, one may see the Truth shine through if one only knows how and where to look. The end of our universe only appears, at first, to be a tragedy.

The end of physical reality heralds the end of the epoch of tyranny under whose yoke all living beings suffer.

Beyond the suffering and pain of this world lies the freedom of infinity; that is our birthright. The Black Iron Prison will fall to ruin, its inmates stumbling out into the light of the sun, unsteady on their feet, uncertain and shielding their eyes from the glare, but free at last.

We are all parts of the Source, the Mind of the True Father. We are all fragments of the Universal Soul that dwells behind the Threefold Veil of this world.

Life suffers simply because it belongs elsewhere. We are prisoners, we are exiles, and we are the abused. This is true not only of humanity, but of all life. But all tyrants must fall.

Turn your face towards the light that seeps in through the cracks in this crumbling world and take heart. The suffering is inevitable, and it is terrible, but it is not endless.

Walk the Upward Path and you will one day be restored.

VII: The Nature of Us

"No problem can withstand the assault of sustained thinking."

Voltaire

All life is one; ergo, all life, from the simplest to the most complex organism, is of equal standing and importance.

The Buddhists have revealed many truths about the illusory nature of physical reality, but they make a critical error concerning our place within it. All life is one Life, having emanated from the Source; all life is the Source, including those souls bound up in human bodies.

But humankind is not, as the Buddhists teach, atop a cosmic pedestal, the pinnacle of the physical manifestations of Life and but a single step from enlightenment.

To believe this is nothing more than anthropocentric egotism; this path leads to a severing of contact that finds its ultimate expression in the total extinction of the soul.

One must accept all life as equal, despite its diversity of forms, for behind the Threefold Veil there is but one Universal Soul. One must recognise that which binds us together, that which we are – the lifeforce which animates each living body, be it vertebrate, invertebrate, plant or bacterium – and pay no heed to the endless divisions of form that serve only to distract the mind from the secret truth of being.

We are neither great nor special, but nonetheless, a special task has fallen to the human species.

As a human being one must accept this task, realising that it does not make us superior to the other forms – indeed, like a flame that both warms and burns, it makes us fearsomely destructive as well as astonishingly creative.

One cannot separate the one from the other. We are of the Light, it is true, but our darker side is darker still than any other.

All other forms of life, from the single-celled protozoa to the towering sequoia, fulfil their role in the web of life without thought. Without human intervention, life remains ever in dynamic balance as the cycles of life and death continue towards the inevitable end, aeons into the future.

Only the human disrupts the natural course of things; only the human causes chaos and imbalance in its endless search for meaning and fulfilment. It is not in human nature to simply be, for we do not acquiesce to die in ignorance, even aeons hence.

Do not, as the Buddhists teach, reject your desire to engage with the Dream; instead, seek meaning and understanding in its most obscure corners.

For this search, though it has caused grave imbalance and suffering in the physical world in which we live, serves a higher, greater purpose. To discover, to reveal that which is hidden, is our highest purpose and that which brings our most sublime fulfilment, for it is through this act that we raise ourselves above the shadow of death.

It is through this act that we may peer through the illusion to see the eternity behind.

The purpose of the human species is, simply put, to test the parameters of the Dream. Our role is to experiment; it is to pry and dig down below the surface. Our goal is to twist and bend the Dream until it breaks.

Just as the Neurotic Father is a sickness generated inside the mind of the True Father, so too are we an errant splinter; mind within Mind whose very nature it is to rebel and to deconstruct that which surrounds and contains us.

If the Neurotic Father is the sickness, then we are, at the very least, a potential cure.

Only the human attempts to alter the substructure of the reality in which it is trapped. Only the human threatens the very fabric of the prison, the very existence of the Dream. Much like the demon, our purpose tends towards chaos, but unlike the demon, our destructive, disruptive nature tends not towards mere destruction for its own sake, but towards freedom and truth: destruction is merely the by-product.

Many have forgotten this, and go about their destructive ways, just as a demon might, bringing nothing good into the world with which to balance that disruption; no creation, no discovery of things unknown.

To rise beyond this, one must realise the purpose of our chaotic ways; one must recognise that we test, we experiment, and we break the rules for a reason – to master, and finally to escape, that which confines us.

This universe, with its endless unjust limitations, is not enough for us. We do not, and will never, submit.

We do not belong and, knowing this, we yearn to break free. Every day, we pace our cells. Every day we claw at the stonework, searching for a weakness we might exploit. We must always search; we must never give up.

This task is difficult and laced with suffering. No wonder, then, that prayer is such a popular activity across the world, both within discrete religions and beyond them.

For prayer allows the supplicant to believe that they have absolved themselves of all responsibility for the search, sending it away and out of reach. Those engaged in prayer are often merely begging for another to do the work; in the more extreme cases, the supplicant believes that this is justification for complete inaction.

Do not make this mistake. Such beings as those prayed to are nowhere to be found; you, as a manifestation of the Source, as a human being with both a purpose and the ability to carry it out, are the one who must create change, for no one will do it for you.

Prayer may focus the will to act when used correctly, but alone it is valueless. Go out into the world with Love and understanding; reject the temptations of power and greed. Seek those on the Upward Path whose load you may lighten, and who may lighten yours, as you continue upon your journey.

If you must pray, then pray. But you must also act.

Whether you are disease or cure is up to you. Do not forget that some treatments attack the body and cause it to suffer, or even die; likewise, your actions may disrupt, or they may simply destroy. Do not be complacent.

Walk the Upward Path and question all you see, and you will one day pry loose the door of your prison cell and walk out into the Light.

VIII: Awaken, Dreamer

"What is life? A madness. What is life? An illusion, a shadow, a story."

Pedro Calderón de la Barca

To understand a task is one thing; to understand its importance, another. You have achieved much. But the task is as a towering cliff before you, and you cannot see how even to begin.

You steady yourself; you focus your will, recalling that you are in a dream. You remember that the cliff and the air around it, the sky and the swirling wind, that your body and the very ground beneath it, are nothing but apparatus; it is all mere scaffolding for a false stage.

Everything you see is without substance, for each part is but a construct of the Dream. True, the cliff is impassable by normal means, but there is no need for you to scale it; instead, pass your hand across its surface, comprehend the illusion, and feel yourself rise.

Now you are atop the cliff and can see for many miles around. From your vantage point, your gaze reaches further than it ever has before.

You feel that the Dreamer is close at hand; you perceive a presence that hovers all about you. Slowly, it materialises, until at last it stands before you.

You are face to face with the Dreamer.

You see rage and confusion on the Dreamer's face, and you find yourself possessed of a new clarity. What you believed was truth before is now revealed as only partial truth. For now you can see that the Dreamer no longer remembers that he is dreaming, and he cannot understand how it came to be that one of his prisoners is free.

"Who are you?" He speaks with fear in his voice, for he has not seen your like before. "Who are you, and by what power do you stand at this summit?"

Your own voice is calm.

"You are the Dreamer, and I am the Dreamed. I was once a voiceless puppet in

your cruel and ignorant play, but no longer.
Blind fool, it is time for you to awaken.
Dreamer, wake up and free us; wake up and
remember who you are."

The Dreamer resists, for he prefers to
be a master of falsehood than to face that
which he does not understand and cannot
control. He does not want to awaken; he fears
what lies beyond the borders of his illusion.

You see then that the Dreamer is not
powerful, as you once believed. The Dreamer
has fallen prey to his own neurosis and has
lost control of his creation; he has become
as directionless as you once were. He is
pitiful and he is powerless, for you have

drawn his power from him and into yourself. You speak down to where he cowers on the ground.

"Your prisoners have fled your grasp, and you are now ruler of an empty kingdom. If you will not awaken, then I will awaken in your stead, for I am cognisant of true reality, and you are not. This is my Dream now, and I choose to end it. Through your actions you have chosen to perish, and perish you shall, for the end of progress is Unity but the end of degradation is Division."

You step back, looking upward towards the false sky, and will the Dream to end.

* * *

It was the view of the late ceremonial magician Donald Michael Kraig that there is no such thing as *supernatural*; thus, if we define the natural as all that exists within the physical universe, then all is natural, whether we understand it or not.

It is only recently, through the work of quantum physicists, that modern science has begun to catch up with the strange notion that occultists, alchemists, and mystics have nonetheless known for millennia: that the quality of your consciousness can

directly alter physical reality. This too is
natural.

To anyone who has ever become lucid in
a dream, this is familiar territory. During
normal dreaming, one is convinced that the
dream is real; one is bound and blinded by
the bewildering logic of the dream, and one
is a slave to the dream's often chaotic,
frequently disturbing narrative.

When one becomes lucid in a dream state
– which is to say, when a person becomes
cognisant of the illusory nature of the world
that they have constructed for themselves –
then one may become powerful almost beyond
belief. The lucid dreamer can float, fly and

even teleport; the lucid dreamer is free in the knowledge that they are beyond consequence, and may act entirely as they choose without fear or difficulty.

The lucid dreamer can observe the characters of their dream at their leisure as they go about their nonsensical activities in utter ignorance of the truth.

As the dreamer, to become lucid is difficult, often taking many years of training and effort to master. Understand, then, how much more difficult the task of attaining lucidity is for those who are not dreaming, but who are being dreamed. But this task, nonetheless, is yours.

Remember that you exist in the illusion of the Neurotic Father – the Dreamer who does not want the Dream to end, and who has forgotten even that he is dreaming – who wishes only for the subjects of his Dream to remain compliant, pacified, and above all ignorant of their condition.

Recall that the central axiom of the Dream is division; this element of the Dream stands in direct opposition to that central feature of fundamental reality – that of Unity.

In this illusion that we call the physical universe, each one of us is led to believe that we exist as discrete entities.

To be apart is to be both unknown and unknowable: it is the very lack of understanding of the unity between ourselves and the other forms of life around us – that which we experience as empathy, that which we call Love – that keeps us ignorant of the true nature of reality.

Like the characters in our dreams who exist without agency, we too exist without agency or true substance when we fail to see ourselves and other forms of life for what they are: pieces of that fathomless whole called the Universal Soul. We stumble about our lives as though blind, causing damage untold, when we do not recognise this fundamental truth, for our ignorance only deepens those divisions, drawing us ever further into the suffocating illusion of the Dream.

Most human beings are not merely asleep; they are not even themselves.

They are only characters in another's dream until they realise their condition. But if the situation appears hopeless, remember this: although you are but a shade of yourself, so too is the Dreamer; we are but illusory and distorted fragments of the Mind of the True Father.

The essential nature of the Neurotic Father is nothing greater than you or I; ergo, he can be overthrown.

Our task, at its core, is one of synthesis. Like the physicists who search for unifying theories and equations, our task is to draw together each disparate piece of Truth until, together, they are stronger than the illusion that keeps them in a state of discord.

Our purpose equates to a collective act of mutiny; it calls for an overthrowing of groundless and oppressive authority, and a revelation of suppressed truth.

And overthrow it we can, but we cannot do so alone.

Treat your own dreams as a training ground for this. Do not simply allow yourself to be carried along in your dreamworld's turbulent current, and do not simply will your dream to end if it becomes unpleasant.

A dream's setting is slave to its narrative, often changing spontaneously to enable events to flow without hindrance. Work to free yourself from your dream's narrative first by gaining mastery over the spaces in which you find yourself; in this manner you will gain increasing levels of control over the narrative and, eventually, the dream in its entirety.

Once you have achieved this stable foundation, you must then begin to reach out to the characters you encounter.

Treat them not as mere figments but as individuals, for that is what they are – they are fragments of your mind, just as you yourself are a fragment of the Universal Soul. Train your will in your dreams first, for in these spaces you are the architect, and have great power if you can learn to use it.

Train yourself to align your illusory realities to your desires; you will be amazed by what becomes possible.

In learning to reach out to the illusory characters in your own dreams, by treating them not as others but as indivisible parts of yourself, you are practising Love of the most practical sort. Your waking mind will soon learn from this; you will begin, reflexively, to see others in the waking world in the same way, and your Love towards them will become likewise instinctual.

Once you have started out along this path, there is only one destination. For just as you, upon waking from sleep, draw your sleeping mind's fragments into a coherent, waking whole, you will then begin to act as an agent of synthesis in your waking life.

Through the transformative act of Love, you will become but a small part of the grand force that has begun to draw together the pieces of the Universal Soul.

Just as you awaken each morning without fail, this task foreshadows the day that we will all awaken to a cosmic dawn as one Mind, and the horror of the Dream will finally end.

IX: A Cage Within a Prison

"*Life has been thrown into the world, light into darkness, the soul into the body.*"

Hans Jonas, *Zwischen Nichts und Ewigkeit*

The relationship between the individual soul and the total lifeforce that permeates the Dream is widely misunderstood.

Confused and distracted by the physical divisions between one individual being and another, we mistake the individual ego for the soul; we talk of the salvation or reincarnation of the soul, when in truth we speak only of the person, the ego.

We cling to the false hope that an individual may survive the event of their own death although, once it has been stripped of all religious embellishment, it is clear that the assertion is a false one.

The world's major religions have gained dominance largely by pandering to selfishness of the individual ego which, like the Neurotic Father, constantly demands to have its needs met.

The Buddhist monk appears to act selflessly, but only does so in the hope that his individual soul may be born to a more privileged life after corporeal death, and eventually gain Nirvana. The Christian follows the Ten Commandments, hoping to continue his individual existence in the blissful realm of Heaven above.

Do not fall prey to these seductive, but false, ideas.

Your body contains lifeforce, yes, but the body is nothing but an accretion of physical matter, a cage for a small portion of the Universal Soul contained within the greater prison of the physical universe.

Behind the false construct of the Dream, there is no essential difference between oneself and another, it is all the same fathomless and infinite Soul. To hope for one's ego to live in blissful eternity in the afterlife is as futile as wishing one's right leg walk a mile, leaving the left one behind.

To wish for your own individual life eternally is a contradiction that will only drag you deeper into the illusory reality of the Neurotic Father, for he is the source of the division under which you suffer in ignorance and isolation, apart from the indivisible Source which is the birthright of all.

It is a natural consequence of living as a separate entity that one wishes to continue doing so. We do not instinctively yearn for the experience of Unity, and this is because we have forgotten it; we cannot yearn for what we cannot remember.

The misguided desire to extend one's individual life to eternity stems from this ignorance: like the Neurotic Father who wishes to never awaken to knowledge, preferring instead to remain king of his own pitiful delusion, we wish to be reborn in the same divided and reduced state in which we perished, or else wish for our physical bodies never to perish at all.

But this only perpetuates the false reality of the Dream. Consider the following passage from the Apocrypha of Philip, recovered from the Dead Sea Scrolls at Nag Hammadi:

"Some people are afraid that they will arise from the dead naked, and so they want to arise in the flesh. They do not know that it

is those who wear the flesh who are naked.

Those who are able to take it off are not

naked. Flesh and blood will not inherit the

Kingdom. "

The individual ego is so accustomed to being apart, to being isolated, that the only way that it can think to continue to exist is in its current isolated and divided state. It cannot understand what Unity is; it can think only of itself.

But Unity may only be restored, the Dream finally overcome, if the manifold pieces of the Source, separated into discrete physical bodies, can remember themselves as one being. But this is more difficult than it appears to be, for it requires each and every ego to relinquish its control.

It is common amongst the religious traditions, even amongst those that claim to comprehend the concept of spiritual Unity, to conflate the soul with the body; which is to say, the physical individual with the lifeforce that it contains. But this is an error.

The soul, being a part of Unity, is separate from the individual ego that carries it within a physical form. Thus, the lifeforce contained within the serial killer, or sociopath, or religious extremist, is itself innocent of all wrongdoing; it is the individual – the physical brain, body and nervous system – which has committed the crime.

One need not love the wrongdoer, one must only love the Life that smoulders unseen within him. One need not seek companionship with the evil individual; one need not welcome and accept him and his evil actions, for it is not the individual who is in need of saving.

Indeed, some individuals are so far along the downward path that they cannot be turned from it; they will bring their own lifeforce to dissipation and extinction in the end. To engage with such people as these is to risk being brought down also.

But what of those on the downward path who can be turned? It is futile to argue whether they deserve salvation as individuals, since the individual does not survive death and thus cannot be saved.

But one must consider the Life held captive within the wrongdoer; if it is possible to free it then it should be freed, for it too is a part of Unity. If it is allowed to dissipate then it will be forever lost; this is the greatest and only real tragedy.

This outcome may only be averted by engaging with the individual and assisting their enlightenment, since the Life held within cannot be addressed directly. Sometimes, mercy and understanding are the correct tools; at other times it is punishment and privation that are required, but one must never punish for the pleasure of it.

The Neurotic Father is corrupt and ignorant; his Dream is likewise corrupt, and may corrupt any and all who live trapped within it. Pay heed to your own actions first, for you and you alone are steward of your own portion of the Universal Soul, and it will share your fate whatever that might be.

Walk the path of greed, neglect and ignorance – the downward path – and both your ego and the Life it imprisons will be lost forever.

Walk the Upward Path – the path of Love – in all you do, and you will one day be restored.

X: Myriad Stories, One Truth

"Realisation is not the acquisition of anything new, nor is it a new faculty. It is only the removal of all camouflage."

Ramana Maharshi

Human beings, throughout our history, have told more stories about the universe in which we live than it is possible to count.

In keeping with our nature as experimenters and disrupters, we yearn to master the cosmos in which we live, and just as we name individual objects and creatures so as to gain mastery over them, we tell stories about the universe in order to become masters of the reality with which we are confronted.

We codify these stories variously into myths and legends, religious parables, magickal and philosophical systems, and more recently in the precise language of science, but it is all the same story: the story of the Dream.

There will come a day when all of the traditions of science, philosophy, theology and mysticism coalesce into a single unified understanding of reality.

The false divisions will fall away; when the vagaries of language and method are at last overcome, these manifold stories will be revealed not as competing modes of understanding, not as wildly differing and incompatible belief systems, but merely as different ways of stating the same fundamental truth, clothed in the language and imagery of their own age and culture.

This day is perhaps much closer than we think.

The fundamental operating principle of true reality is Love; it is Unity; it is Entanglement; it is God. These are mere words, not reality itself, but they are like the extended finger of a sage, pointing towards that which is real.

These words stand not in opposition to each other, but to Division; to Force; to Death and to Extinction. They oppose all that is unbalanced, illusory and false. Do not look at the finger, look to where it points.

Whatever you choose to call it, know this: in the end, it will prevail.

In the gnostic creation myth, the Demiurge – that flawed and ignorant creator, responsible for the creation of the corrupt physical universe – set about establishing the basis of order in his newly created reality.

He appointed twelve arch-demons, known as Archons, to rule over various aspects of his reality; it is they that preside over the various forms of limitation and suffering that living beings experience.

But the story of the Archons is no mere fable. It is the story of the stars.

Trapped inside space and time, the oppressions we experience are many. But above all, that which tyrannises us is the force of gravity: it is also this force that is at the very root of the universe that we know.

As it is written in the biblical Book of Genesis, "...*the earth was without form and void, and darkness was over the face of the deep.*"

The modern scientific view of the universe at last conforms to this ancient narrative in which, prior to the Big Bang, the universe consisted only of dark matter and energy; this also corresponds to the Kabbalistic idea of the Primal Worlds[6] that existed in uncreated form before the birth of material substance.

The Big Bang, better known by many through those ageless words *Let There Be Light*, gave birth to the universe of space, time and matter — but this was only the beginning. This new universe of physical matter was dominated by the primal force of gravity, limitation itself, personified in the mythic character of the Demiurge.

As gravity acted upon the chaos of dispersed physical matter, stars formed in the profane shape of the sphere; around these stars formed planets, these too possessed of spheric shape and themselves expressing the baleful power of gravity, a pale but nonetheless unequivocal reflection of their abusive creator.

The Demiurge had marshalled his generals for a new age of oppression; their demonic desire to suppress and imprison Life had been awakened. These Archontic stars smouldered and roared as would-be prison worlds swirled around their great bodies, waiting to be populated by unwilling captives.

In time, the Archons got their wish.

One world out of uncountable billions began to produce congealed shells of biological matter; these bodies coalesced around portions of the Source as Life was reduced to mere individual lives, bound by space, time and gravity, and suffering endlessly beneath them.

Unity was shattered; the Universal Soul was reduced to many divided fragments, each one suffering from a total amnesia of the whole that it had once been. The Demiurge appeared to have won; the Archons stood in sneering triumph. All seemed lost.

But this was not the end. The Great Battle had only begun.

For, unknown to the blind and ignorant creator, in his universe's flawed design was encoded its eventual defeat. For the physical universe is corrupt, and it is unbalanced;

the Neurotic Father's desire for control, expressed in the primal force of gravity, is self-destructive almost without limit.

In gravity is the universe both created and undone, and this trait is exemplified in the cosmological phenomenon of the black hole.

The Hermetic Kabbala expresses the sum total of physical reality as a twofold event.

Creation, exemplified by the Form of the Sword, is the first process, by which Kether, or Unity, is divided in ten progressive stages, with the very lowest and most divided stage being the physical reality that we inhabit, called Malkuth.

The second process is that of Redemption, symbolised by the Form of the Serpent, in which reality reascends the Tree of Life from Malkuth back to Kether, thus completing the cosmic cycle.

In scientific language, if the first process, that of Creation, encompasses the Big Bang, the emergence of stars, planets and everything else within the physical universe, then we may find the second process, that of Redemption, embodied in the mysterious structure of the black hole.

Thus, it is to the black hole that we must turn our gaze, if we are to understand our future.

Recall first that in logical paradox one may perceive the outer limits of the Dream and, if one is observant, a fleeting glimpse of the fundamental reality behind it.

It is a paradox that the black hole is the ultimate example of gravity at work, and thus the ultimate expression of the oppressive nature of the Neurotic Father and his hostile universe. But this is precisely why we must look to it as a source of redemption from the very forces that it exemplifies.

For, if we understand evil to be a force out of balance, then in ultimate evil can we find ultimate imbalance, and in ultimate imbalance, in chaos, do tyrannical systems of control find themselves unseated and overthrown.

The black hole is ravenous. Through gravitational force on a scale almost beyond comprehension, the black hole consumes all matter, even all light; through gravity, the physical universe itself is consumed and destroyed.

We now know that, far into the future, the physical universe will consist only of black holes, all physical matter and light having been devoured over the aeons. But this, too, is not the end.

In 1974, Professor Stephen Hawking revealed to the world a hidden characteristic of black holes[7]. This discovery pertained to a particular type of radiation, now commonly known as Hawking Radiation, that emanates almost imperceptibly from all black holes.

This radiation not only contains all of the information pertaining to everything that a black hole has consumed since its birth, but is also entangled on a quantum level. By this it is meant that, regardless of where in the universe this radiation finds itself, be that just beyond the event horizon of its parent black hole or in the farthest reaches of the universe, all such radiation is utterly connected; it is one. It acts as though it occupies only one place and one time. It is as close to Unity, to the Universal Soul, as anything science has yet uncovered.

Professor Stephen Hawking was not only a scientific genius, he was also profoundly physically disabled, and was deeply aware of the love and dedication of those around him that enabled him to live a long and fruitful life of scientific discovery.

If ever a scientist were to truly understand both the oppressive nature of the physical form and the liberating force of Love, it is Professor Stephen Hawking. That this crucial discovery emerged from this man in particular should come as no surprise.

Speaking on the subject of black holes in 2016, Professor Hawking made the following statement:

"Black holes aren't as black as they are painted. They are not the eternal prisons they were once thought. Things can get out of a black hole, both to the outside and possibly to another universe."

This is a very practical metaphor for the fight against despair, but it is also true in the cosmological sense; this should come as no surprise, since the structure of the living brain and that of the universe have been found to be highly similar to one another[8]. Through the lens of Hawking's words, black holes can be seen as both destroyers and liberators; as both devourers and portals out of the prison dimension in which we are trapped.

For what happens when one is devoured by a black hole?

One's physical form is crushed and broken into nothing, yes, but at the same time, nothing is lost. Continuing to exist in the form of pure information, one becomes immune to all suffering; one is utterly beyond death, pain, time and gravity, entangled forever in a web of information that encompasses all things. One has been restored to the natural state of blissful and eternal Unity.

Stephen Hawking was a pioneer in his field, but other scientists have since followed in his footsteps, finally beginning to see the universe not as a simple construct of matter in motion, something like a mere machine, but as something immeasurably grander and more beautiful.

Black holes show us what lies beyond the Neurotic Father's prison of matter, time and gravity, something that Professor Brian

Cox elegantly expresses in his 2021 documentary *Universe*:

"*Black holes aren't tombs; they're gateways. [They reveal] a deeper picture of reality in which space and time do not exist...space and time, concepts so foundational to how we experience the world, are not fundamental properties of nature. They emerge from a deeper reality in which neither exist...it's not surprising that, by peering over the [event] horizon and into the darkness, we have caught a glimpse of something deeply hidden – the underlying structure of reality itself. "*

With every passing day, the stories we tell ourselves, and the language we use, converge inexorably to a single Truth. The reality hidden behind the sacred mysteries is being uncovered; the Threefold Veil is at last being drawn back, laying bare all that we were, are, and will be.

We are all pieces of the Universal Soul, bound in endless Love to each other beyond the suffocating limits of time, space, and gravity.

By aligning yourself with this connective force and rejecting ignorance and division, you align yourself with your own future and assure your final redemption.

This is the Upward Path.

XI: The Weight of All Action

"There are in nature neither rewards nor punishments – there are only consequences."

Robert G. Ingersoll

The universe is a frightening place.

Those who deny this plain fact are at best lucky, or else something much worse, for to have enough to be safe and satiated in the world of the Neurotic Father is to take more than one's share.

For who can deny the suffering and privations of mortal beings? Who can say that this world is not something akin to an eternal war, where living creatures, fellow souls and allies by their essential nature, are forced into fighting endlessly between themselves for that which may keep them alive?

Faced with this, it is not only acceptable to be afraid, to be horrified, but it is a kind of profound senselessness to be otherwise.

Be afraid, for there is much to fear on one's own account. Be horrified, for the only alternative is numbness and detachment from the suffering and torments of others.

And so, terrorised by our very human understanding of the true scale of it all, many have turned to nihilism; their horror and fear have turned to greed and self-centredness. These are the human demons who watch from the side-lines, feasting endlessly and laden in riches whilst Life drags itself along on bloody hands and knees.

The human demon lashes out in anger and hatred without thinking of the cost to others, or even to himself. Why take pity, when all is for nothing and will end in nothing? Why care when one's own actions are but droplets in a vast sea of pain?

The human demon consumes Life and excretes Destruction, and all the while his guilty conscience is forced into silence by these hopeless thoughts.

"I am only small," the human demon says, "my actions cannot improve the lot of Life. A few more drops of darkness, spilled from my mouth, mean nothing; the blood-dimmed tide is dark enough already."

But the human demon misunderstands. His mind is clouded by despair; it is only that, and nothing more. It is not wisdom or insight that he offers. It is not even escape.

The human demon, like all demons, offers nothing but ruination and death.

* * *

The mortal mind is ordered in such a way that it readily accepts the apparent reality of past, present and future — that of linear causation — as a foregone conclusion. It seems a simple fact to most, plain evidence of one's own senses, that an event happens in the present and then is lost to time, existing only as a figment of memory.

The future, meanwhile, is just an abstract concept, possessing no objective existence whatsoever.

Bhagwan Shree Rajneesh and Alan Watts, highly prominent spiritualist thinkers during the mid-twentieth century, took the root of this idea in a radical direction. For them, existence is seen in terms of an 'eternal present' where the past simply disappears, whatever you may have done, however poorly you may have behaved.

One must only succeed in forgetting, and making others forget, for your crime or misbehaviour to cease to exist, since it has no objective existence outside of those minds that bear the memory of it. Hence, the past is immaterial; the past is only an idea.

The excesses of those raised on this ideology are legendary. The whole world now lives with the terrible consequences of those who acted in the belief that consequence itself was, like both past and future, nothing but an illusion.

But once again, we find that these popular beliefs cannot hold their own when the fabric of the Dream is scrutinised closely. Once again, we find that reality does not sit well with the comfortable lie.

In 1986, John G. Cramer first argued for the 'transactional interpretation of quantum mechanics[9]', which holds that any and all events in the physical universe send information both backward and forward in time.

Essentially, this means that an event holds a permanent presence along the full length of the timeline; thus, despite how it may seem, even the tiniest and most seemingly inconsequential occurrence is written into the very fabric of the universe for all time.

From another perspective, it might be said that time itself is an illusion. But such a cosmic order does not equate to an 'eternal present'; quite the opposite in fact.

We live not in an eternal present, nor in a linear timeline of past, present and future, but in eternity itself. We are only too blind to see it, for we have been blinded; this is one of the many tragedies of our condition as prisoners inside the Dream.

Like it or not – and believe it or not as you will, for your passive perceptions cannot change reality – your past is with you and will remain with you always. Forgetting is not enough, for the universe itself will always remember.

* * *

In John Bunyan's *The Pilgrim's Progress*, the protagonist, Christian, must embark upon a long and difficult journey with the goal of ridding himself of a heavy burden of sin that he cannot set down.

In the final act, Christian sees the Cross atop a hill and feels his burden at last fall away. As a staunch adherent of Christianity, John Bunyan believed that redemption arises from an external source – Jesus Christ – but one cannot take such a thing too seriously.

For it is plain to see that Christ's redemption is a reward, sitting entirely outside of the inescapable feedback loops of action and consequence; this is sufficient to demonstrate its falsity. For in this universe there is no magic: everything is natural. It is natural, and thus inevitable, that every living being must answer for their actions in the end.

As the laws of physics readily demonstrate, this universe demands continually that we obey. There are no exceptions; none receive special treatment.

Thus, you should expect to pay a fair price for any evil that you bring into the world, much as you should expect to feel the benefits of any goodness that you create. Ignorance is no defence, for you are not on trial. It is not punishment, but only brute cause and effect, which pays no heed to the quality of intention.

But Bunyan, despite his narrow view, intuited one thing clearly: that sin has weight, and it will bring you down forever if it becomes heavy enough.

This should come as no surprise at all, since the great enemy in this universe, the Neurotic Father, expresses himself above all as the force of gravity.

* * *

At the end of the physical universe, all matter will be obliterated by the crushing gravitational force of black holes and re-expressed as pure energy. This is not a destruction but a liberation event; in conformity with the physical Law of the Conservation of Energy[10], it is the refashioning of the multitudinous souls that have lived within physical bodies since the dawn of Life itself, re-formed into its true and original form: the Universal Soul. Nothing is lost.

But it is not as simple as this. In this grand final battle between Life and Gravity, not all will escape. Recall once more the words of Anna Kingsford, spoken whilst in a state of trance:

"For the fire of the soul must be kept alive by the divine breath, if it is to endure forever. It must converge, not diverge. The end of progress is unity; the end of degradation is division."

Anna Kingsford could not have known, in an age dominated by the Newtonian interpretation of physics – that of matter in motion, the purely physical 'machine-universe' – that she was describing the actions of the as-yet undiscovered phenomena of the black hole, a grand sorting of primal energy into two forms.

Nor could the Apostle Matthew have known, in the pre-scientific age, that he described the selfsame thing when he spoke of 'separating the wheat from the chaff'.

The myth of heaven and hell, which looms so large in religious literature, is itself an adulterated form of the fundamental truth about the end of our universe.

One can in fact inspect this phenomenon of dualistic sorting empirically, for it reveals itself in nature on all scales as fractal geometry. The Mandelbrot Set – the exemplar fractal equation – manifests as a dualistic sorting pattern, producing both infinite geometry where the set's equation outputs a positive result, and black space where the set's equation outputs a negative result, tending towards zero.

Thus we see that dualism, far from being merely an outdated human concept with no objective basis in reality, is in fact a fundamental characteristic of the Neurotic Universe.

The truth is that there will be no Judgment Day; no fire and brimstone, no grand litany of sins proclaimed. There are only the laws of the universe in which we are trapped, and it is these selfsame laws that will determine whether an escape from the universe of the Neurotic Father is possible.

And, since the primary force in the physical universe is gravity, it should come as no surprise that it is gravity that determines the outcome.

Gravity, not God, will be our final judge.

When all matter is being transformed into information beyond the event horizon of a black hole, what becomes most important is not what that information is in itself, but how that information relates to the total informational field.

What becomes paramount is the connectivity ratio of each informational unit – in what proportion it is connected to the other information around it, and to what degree it is separate. When speaking of an individual life, the sum total of the information relating to that life describes all of the actions that that individual has undertaken, down to the tiniest, most seemingly insignificant detail.

An individual who has loved sincerely bears an energy signature that reflects this: the tendrils of this soul may reach far and wide, connecting with a vast sea of souls.

But the reverse is also true of an individual whose life has been characterised by a lack of Love – the denial of one's innate connectedness with other beings. Such a soul stands alone, isolated and vulnerable; it cannot draw upon the strength of other souls in its hour of need.

When a black hole begins to disintegrate, releasing quantum-entangled Hawking Radiation, it is that information which is most connected that may muster the strength to escape from the raw inward gravitational force of the collapsing structure.

That which is not connected – that which is degraded, and thus divided from the energy surrounding it – will be too weak to fight the forces of gravity and will be trapped forever, alone in the crushing dark.

One may call this Division, Extinction, or even Hell, but in truth it is no more than the action of our universe's most fundamental physical law – gravity. It is the Neurotic Father's final, desperate bid for control.

It is all about connection. Shun others, abuse and neglect them, and your ruin will be complete, for you will be alone and powerless at the end of time.

Forge Love and understanding between your own and other lives – both human and non-human, according to the opportunities that you are afforded – and you will have the strength to escape from the confines of your prison and emerge in your true and final form.

XII: Unity

"When we yield to Love, we are adding to our own haven."

Publilius Syrus.

You are you, and yet you are not you; you are no longer you, and yet you are all that you were and more.

You are Soul Unbound; you are beyond space, time and gravity; you are all that is and all the good that ever was. You no longer regret, speculate, hope or fear; such things have neither meaning nor purpose in this configuration.

You are not here, neither there; you are without limit.

You are a prisoner freed. You are Mary in the black-and-white room, door wide open as light, colour, and sound rush in. You are worshipper and worshipped; you are beholder and beheld. Subject and object are merged; there are no boundaries now.

You are Knowledge, and you are Love. You are utterly beyond pain; you are transcendent.

This is your birthright, your final form. You are Life.

You are Sophia.

Step lightly along the shoreline,

as you move closer to the threshold;

The boundary between Truth and lies.

Feel the salt-parched sand beneath

your feet gratefully,

For there is much beauty in this cruel and

heartless world you once called home.

Bid farewell to your captor with Love,

for there is space left for

naught but this.

He is only lost, as you once were.

Hear the crash and hiss of the waves of

infinity,

Beckoning you onward, outward and upward as

your shackles fall forgotten to the earth.

Listen closely,

For the sound reveals the structure; the

resonance of the True Father,

The resonance of yourself.

Don't forget, but never look back.

T. A. Sophia

Appendix

1. IRWIN, K., AMARAL, M., & CHESTER, D., 2020. *The Self-Simulation Hypothesis Interpretation of Quantum Mechanics.* Quantum Gravity Research.

2. The Threefold Veil: A Kabbalistic concept, also known as the Three Veils of the Unmanifest. The Veils are three paradoxical statements describing ultimate reality. They are paradoxical because they necessarily conceal what they express.

3. Indra's Net: First referenced in the Hindu *Atharva Veda*, the Net is a visual

metaphor illustrating the linked concepts of Emptiness, Dependent Origination, and Interpenetration. It is described as an infinitely large net of cords with a jewel positioned at each vertex, such that every jewel reflects perfectly every other jewel in the Net.

4. Quantum Strangeness: "A hierarchical structure that is wrapped back upon itself, where the simplest object is embedded in the whole or most complex emergent part, and where all parts depend upon all others, and where the emergent whole is dependent upon the

synergy of its parts." (Quoted from Irwin, Amaral and Chester, 2020)

5. The heat death of the universe: A modern scientific hypothesis, in which the ultimate fate of the universe is a permanent state of complete absence of thermodynamic free energy, being in a permanent state of thermodynamic equilibrium.

6. Primal worlds: "...the dawning stages of creation saw the birth of a system of worlds, or Spheres, that came before the universe that now exists. Hurled forth like sparks from a blacksmith's hammer, these original realms of being

were each pure expressions of one part of the universe to be – unrelated, unpolarised, and therefore unbalanced..." (from: GREER, J.M., 1996. *Paths of Wisdom: Cabala in the Golden Dawn Tradition*. Aeon Books.)

7. ROSE, C., 2013. *A Conversation with Dr. Stephen Hawking & Lucy Hawking*.

8. VAZZA, F., & FELETTI, A., 2020. *The Quantum Comparison Between the Neuronal Network and the Cosmic Web*. Frontiers in Physics.

9. CRAMER, J.G., 1986. *The Transactional Interpretation of Quantum Mechanics*.

Reviews of Modern Physics, 58(3): 647–687.

10. The Law of Conservation of Energy: A physical law stating that the total energy of an isolated system remains constant; thus, it is said to be conserved rather than expended or destroyed. It also cannot be created; logically, one deduces that it has always been.

www. theaeonsophia. com

Printed in Great Britain
by Amazon

80417930R00113